Lisa Murphy.

NAMES

Sue Benton

HODDER AND STOUGHTON
LONDON SYDNEY AUCKLAND TORONTO

We are surrounded by names wherever we look – street names, place names, advertisements, brand names, names of cars, newspapers, shop signs – you name it. They may tell us about ourselves and our history, about our dreams and how we like to see ourselves. In some ways names shape our world.

How many names can you find in the picture?
Make a list of them under different headings:

- names of *people*
- names of *places*
- names of *things that are for sale*.

Any others?

Could you exchange the names in any one list for the names in any other – for example, could you call a cinema *The Sidebottom*? Some will fit quite easily, others may seem very odd. In groups discuss why this is so.

Try to draw a similar picture of an area you know well near your home or your school and include all the names you can find, in the same way. If you are not keen on drawing, you could take a photograph, or just make a list of the names.

The pictures and lists could make a display and, like the picture above, could make your own starting point for talking and thinking about names.

FIRST NAMES

In this poem, which was written in 1809, the little girl who speaks it has been asked to choose a name for her new baby sister.

Now I wonder what would please her,
Charlotte, Julia or Louisa?
Ann and Mary, they're too common;
Joan's too formal for a woman:
Jane's a prettier name beside;
But we had a Jane that died.
They would say, if 'twas Rebecca,
That she was a little Quaker,
Edith's pretty, but that looks
Better in old English books.
Ellen's left off long ago:
Blanche is out of fashion now.
None that I have named as yet
Are so good as Margaret.
Emily is neat and fine.
What do you think of Caroline?

How I'm puzzled and perplexed
What to choose or think of next!
I am in a little fever
Lest the name that I shall give her
Should disgrace her or defame her.
I will leave Papa to name her.

Charles Lamb

In a group make a list of the things which the girl thought about when trying to choose a name for her sister.

Add to your list any other things you think are important when choosing a name; such as whether it sounds right with the surname, or whether the child is to be named after someone in the family or someone famous.

Who chose *your* name and what did they think about before deciding?

Is there anything you dislike about your own names? If you could choose new names for yourself, what would you choose? Now test the new name out by trying the Name Game on p. 10.

First names tend to go in fashions. The little girl in the poem opposite thought Ellen and Blanche were old-fashioned. Names such as Agnes, Gertrude or Cyril, which were popular early in this century, are hardly used now. Other names like Darren, Craig or Tracey did not appear in the lists of the most popular names until the 1970s.

Each year various surveys are done to see which are the most used names: one is based on all the families called Smith and how they have named their children every year since 1921; another is based on the 'Births' column in *The Times* newspaper. On pages 6–9 you will find the list of the top forty boys' names and the top forty girls' names for 1980, based on the Smith lists.

You can conduct your own survey into first name fashions. Ask your teacher for a list of the children in your year at school and work out which were the most popular names about the time you were born.

First names can be put into several groups. Some were descriptions, often from Greek, Latin or Gaelic words, for example Philip (Greek, 'lover of horses'), Paul (Latin, 'small') or Fiona (Gaelic, 'fair/white').

People often give their children names from the Bible or the names of saints. This is not as common as it used to be, but Roman Catholics usually give their children the name of a saint as one of their names, so that each child will have a saint to take a special interest in its welfare.

Some first names were invented by writers for characters in their books. Examples of these are Pamela and Lorna.

Place names have also given us some of our common first names: for example Douglas (dark blue, from a river name), Craig (a crag) and Shirley (bright clearing).

Look up the meanings and origins of your own names, using the list of the top fifty names on pages 6–9. If your name is not on the list you will need to use reference books in your classroom or in a library.

Top forty girls' names for 1980

	Name	Other spellings included	Language it came from	Usual source	Meaning
1	Emma		Old German		'whole' or 'universal'
2	Claire	Clare, Clair	Latin		'bright' or 'clear'
3	Sarah	Sara	Hebrew	Bible	'princess'
4	Kelly	Kelley, Kellie, Kelli	Irish	place name or surname	
5	Rebecca	Rebekah	Hebrew	Bible	'heifer'
6	Lisa	Liza	Hebrew	short form of Elizabeth	'God is satisfaction'
7	Nicola	Nichola	Greek	feminine form of Nicholas	see Nicholas
8	Laura		Latin	feminine form of Lawrence	'person from Laurentum'
9	Rachel	Rachael, Rachele, Rachelle	Hebrew	Bible	'a ewe'
10	Victoria		Latin	Royal family	'victory'
11	Catherine	Kathryn, Katherine, Kaitlin, Katharine, Caitlin, Cathlyn	Greek	saint	'pure'
12	Joanne	Jo-Anne	Hebrew	Bible, feminine form of John	see John
12	Louise	Luis	French	feminine form of Louis	'famous battle'
14	Kerry	Kerrie, Kerri, Keri	Irish	place name	
15	Natalie	Nathalie	Latin		'Christmas Day'
16	Michelle	Michele	Hebrew	feminine form of Michael	'who is like the Lord'
17	Katie	Katy, Kaetie, Catie	Greek	short form of Catherine	see Catherine
18	Helen		Greek		'the bright one'
19	Jennifer		Cornish (Welsh)	Cornish form of Guinevere	?
20	Lindsay	Lyndsey, Lynsey, Linsey, Lindsey, Lyndsay, Linzi	English	place name and surname	'Lincoln island'

21	Donna	Donnah	Italian		'lady'
22	Leanne	Leann, Leeanne, Lee-Anne, Leigh-Ann, Leighanne, Lleanne	Latin	blend of Lea and Anne, or reshaping of Leonie, feminine form of Leo	'lion'
23	Caroline	Carolyn, Carolyne, Carroline, Karilyn	Italian (Germanic)	Italian feminine form of Charles	Charles = 'a man'
23	Samantha		Aramaic (Syrian)		'listener'
25	Charlotte		French (Italian)	French feminine form of Italian Carlo	as for Caroline
26	Amy	Ami, Amie	Old French		'loved'
26	Tracy	Tracey	Greek	pet form of Theresa, also surname	'reaper'
28	Alison	Allison, Alyson	French (Old German)	short form of Alice	'nobility'
28	Gemma	Jemma	Italian		'gem'
28	Jodie	Jody, Jodi, Jodee	Hebrew	form of Judith	'Jewess'
31	Amanda		Latin		'lovable'
32	Deborah	Debra	Hebrew		'a bee'
32	Emily	Emilie, Emilly	Latin		'to excel'
32	Hayley	Hailie	Old English	place name and surname	'high clearing'
35	Karen	Keren	Danish	Danish form of Catherine	see Catherine
36	Melanie	Melloney	Greek		'black'
37	Carly	Carlie, Karlie, Karly	Italian	short form of Carla, feminine form of Charles	see Caroline
37	Lucy		Latin	form of Lucia, feminine form of Lucian	?
39	Kate		Greek	short form of Catherine	see Catherine
40	Paula		Latin	feminine form of Paul	'small'

Top forty boys' names for 1980

	Name	Other spellings included	Language it came from	Usual source	Meaning
1	Matthew	Mathew, Mattthew	Hebrew	saint	'gift of Jehovah (God)'
2	David		Hebrew	saint	'friend'
2	Paul	Ppaul	Latin	Bible	'small'
4	Stephen	Steven	Greek	Bible	'crown'
5	Daniel		Hebrew	Bible	'God has judged'
6	Mark	Marc	Latin	Bible	named after Mars, the Roman god of war
7	Andrew		Greek	Bible	'manly'
8	Christopher	Kristofer, Chrstopher, Kristifor	Greek	saint	'carrying Christ'
9	Michael		Hebrew	Bible	'he who is like the Lord'
10	James		Latin	saint, and Latin form of Jacob	Jacob (Hebrew) 'heel'
10	Lee	Leigh (usually female spelling)	Old English	surname	'dweller by the wood or clearing'
12	Robert		Old English, Norman and Old German		'bright fame'
13	Richard		Old English, Norman and Old German		'stern ruler'
14	Adam		Hebrew	Bible	'red skin'
15	Darren	Daren, Darran	?	possibly surname	meaning and origin uncertain
16	Jonathan	Johnathan, Jonathon	Hebrew	Bible	'Jehovah (God) has given'
17	Craig		Middle English	surname	'dweller by the crag'
18	Peter		Greek	Bible	'stone'
19	Neil		Irish/Gaelic		'champion'
19	Philip	Phillip	Greek	Bible	'lover of horses'

21	Simon		Hebrew	Bible	Biblical form of Simeon meaning 'obedient' (in Greek Simon means 'snub-nosed')
22	Carl	Karl	Old English and German		'a man'
23	Anthony	Antony	Latin	saint	?
23	Stuart	Stewart	Old English	surname	'steward'
23	Thomas		Aramaic (Syrian)	Bible	'twin'
26	Benjamin		Hebrew	Bible	'son of the south' i.e. 'son of the right hand'
27	Gary	Garry	Norman and Old German or Welsh	short form of Gerard or Gareth	'firm spear' 'old man'
27	John	Jon	Hebrew	Bible and saint	'God has favoured'
29	Kevin	Kevyn	Celtic	Saint	'comely birth'
30	Dean		Old English	surname	'person who lives in a valley'
30	Ian	Iain, Iaian	Gaelic	Gaelic form of John	see John
32	Jason		Greek (Hebrew)	Bible	Greek translation of Hebrew 'healer'
33	Alan	Allan, Allen	Celtic and Norman		?
34	Martin	Martyn	Latin	Saint	'follower of Mars'
35	Gareth	Garath	Welsh	Welsh form of Gerontius	'old man'
36	Wayne	Wayn	Old English	surname	'waggon maker'
37	Nicholas	Nicolas	Greek	Saint	'victory of the people'
38	Oliver		Old French/ Norman		'olive tree'
39	Gavin		Celtic and Germanic	German form of Celtic Gawain	'white hawk'
40	Jamie		Scottish	Scottish short form of James	see James

The Name Game

Have you ever helped to choose a name for a baby brother or sister or cousin? Have your ever wished your parents had chosen differently for you? Do you like your name? Would you like to change it? Here's your chance to try choosing a name.

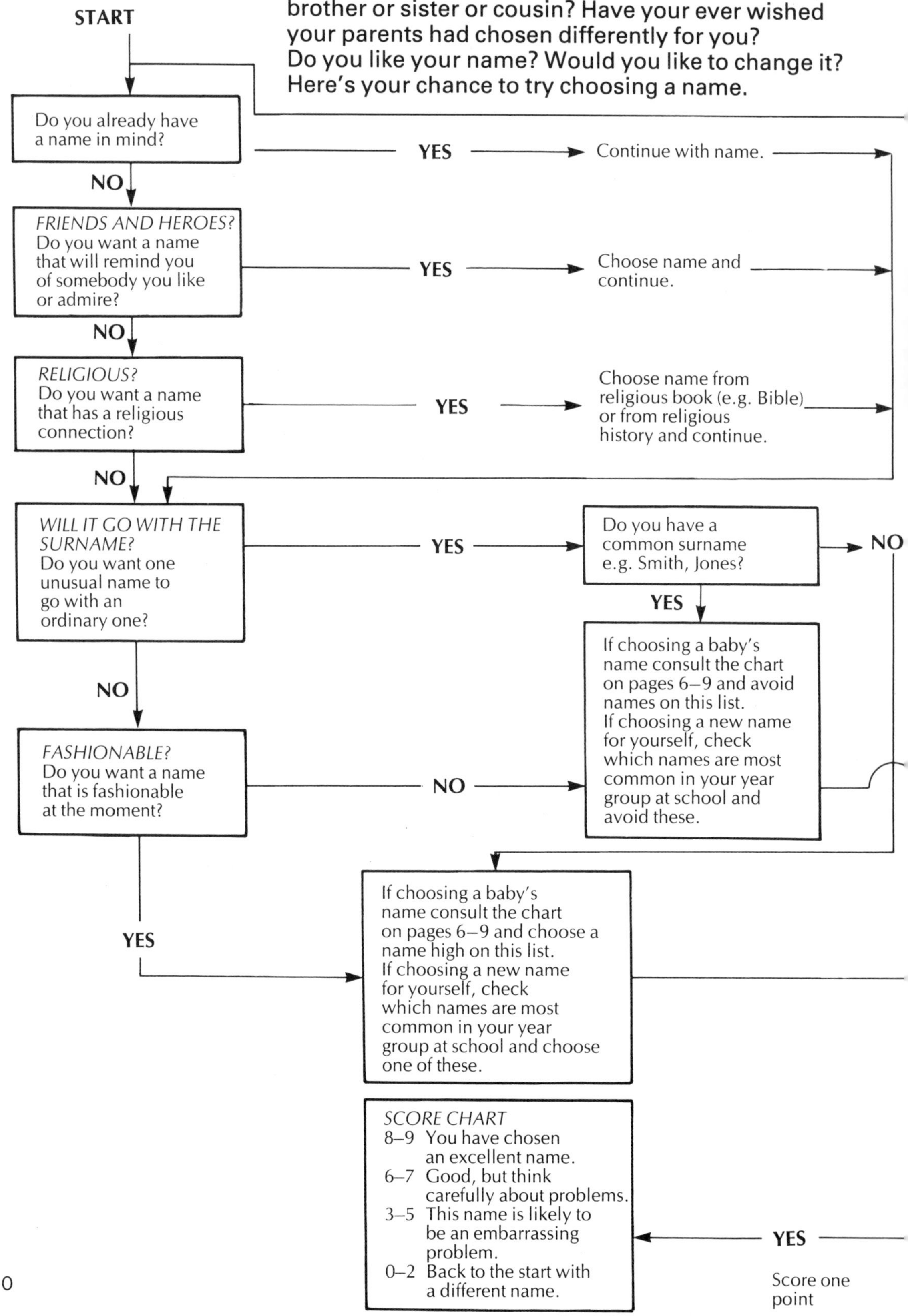

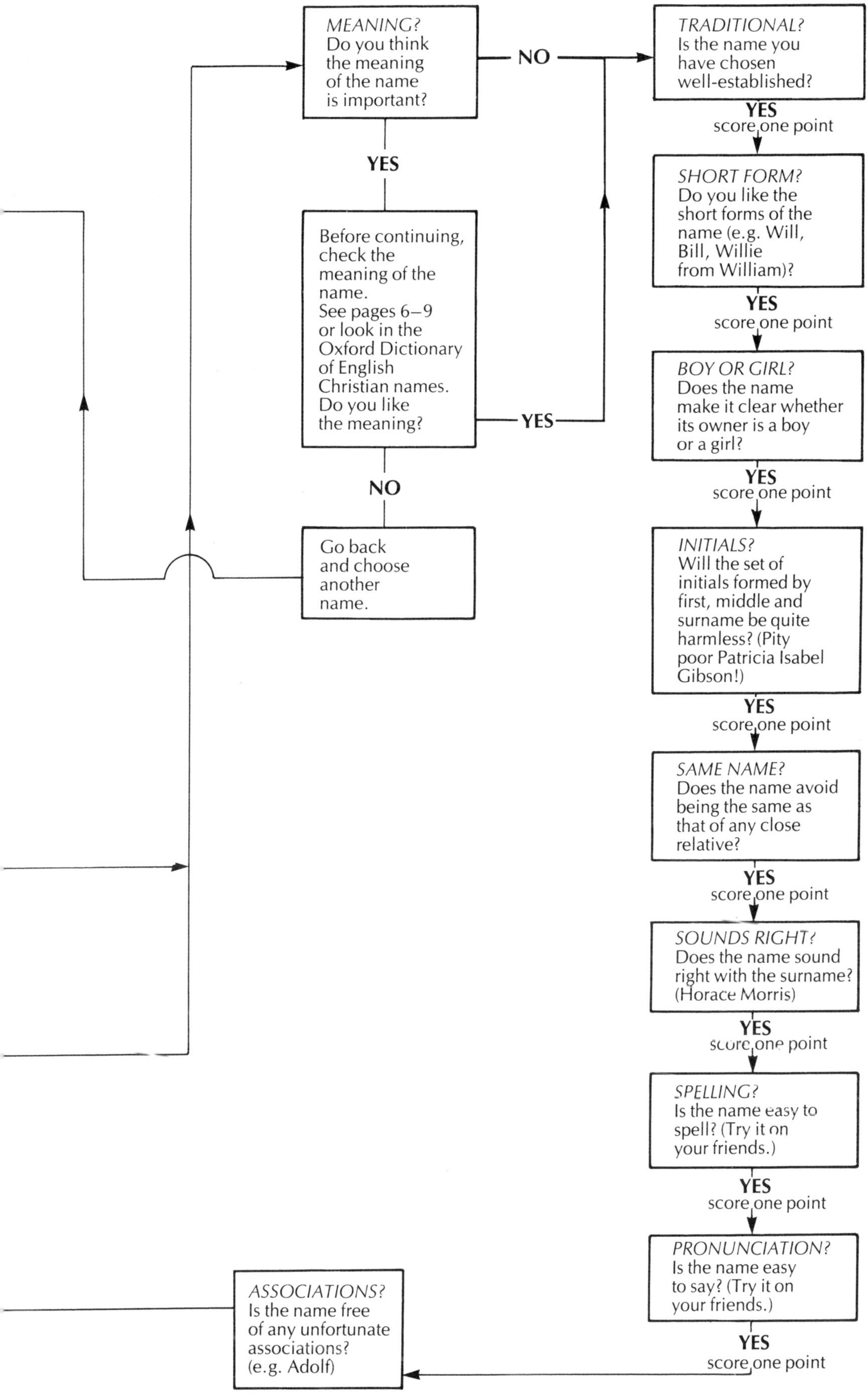
MEANING? Do you think the meaning of the name is important?
NO
YES
Before continuing, check the meaning of the name. See pages 6–9 or look in the Oxford Dictionary of English Christian names. Do you like the meaning?
YES
NO
Go back and choose another name.
TRADITIONAL? Is the name you have chosen well-established?
YES score one point
SHORT FORM? Do you like the short forms of the name (e.g. Will, Bill, Willie from William)?
YES score one point
BOY OR GIRL? Does the name make it clear whether its owner is a boy or a girl?
YES score one point
INITIALS? Will the set of initials formed by first, middle and surname be quite harmless? (Pity poor Patricia Isabel Gibson!)
YES score one point
SAME NAME? Does the name avoid being the same as that of any close relative?
YES score one point
SOUNDS RIGHT? Does the name sound right with the surname? (Horace Morris)
YES score one point
SPELLING? Is the name easy to spell? (Try it on your friends.)
YES score one point
PRONUNCIATION? Is the name easy to say? (Try it on your friends.)
YES score one point
ASSOCIATIONS? Is the name free of any unfortunate associations? (e.g. Adolf)

Many first names have playground rhymes about them.

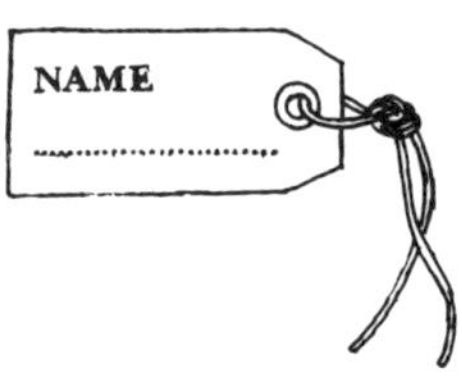

Write down any rhymes you know about particular names. Put your list together with those written by other people to make a class collection.

People often reply to these name rhymes by chanting:

> Sticks and stones may break my bones
> But names will never hurt me.
> When I'm dead and in my grave
> You'll be sorry for what you've called me.

But as Brian Lee says in the following poem, names may sometimes hurt more than we let people know.

Words

Sticks and stones
May break my bones
But words can never hurt me –
That is what I'm supposed to say.

But:
'One, two, three,
Bri-an Lee –
His mother picks his fleas,
She roasts them,
She toasts them,
They have them for their teas.'

Sticks and stones
May break my bones
But words can never hurt me –
That is what I say.

But:
'One, two, three,
Bri-an Lee
Went to sea –
A big fish swam up
Got him by the knee.
The boat turned over
Brian couldn't swim
I wonder whatever
Happened to him.'

Sticks and stones
May break my bones
But . . .

'One, two, three,
Bri-an Lee
Went for a pee –
Never came back.
Found him later
Put him in a sack.'

Sticks and stones . . .

But . . .
Words can prick
Can pierce, can sting,
Can cut, can stab
Can scar, can cling:
This is what I shout back –

'Georgie Rudden
Is fat as a pig
He eats so much pudden
His belly gets big.'

'Mary McVickers'
Brain's gone numb
When she bends over
We can all see her bum.
She's forgot to put them on –
No-nickers
Mary McVickers.'

'Freddie Bell
's got feet that smell –
He won't change his socks.
Shut him in a cell,
Drop him down a well,
Nail him in a box.'

But . . .
Nothing I say
Is ever good enough
To hurt them as much
As they hurt me,
Though we stand and shout
Till someone comes out
And tells us to clear off.

Sticks and stones
May break my bones –
With a pound of plaster
Your bones get better –

But once it's been heard,
Who forgets the Word?

Read through the poem in a small group. You could read it out loud with one person reading Brian Lee's part and the rest of the group reading the others who are baiting him.

At the end of the poem, Brian Lee says that words hurt more than broken bones. In your group, discuss *why* he says this and whether you think it is true.

Do some people get called names whereas others don't? If this is so, why do you think it happens?

How do you think the victim of the name calling feels? Look back at the poem and see how Brian Lee feels.

On your own, try to remember a time when other people called you names and write about it. Make sure you describe what happened, how you felt and what you did about it.

Or, write a story about a child who is called names by the others, explaining how the child feels and how he, or she, reacts to this.

When a new child joins a class or group he or she often does not want to give his or her name for fear of teasing. There are several rhymes to avoid answering the question 'What's your name?'

What's your name?
Mary Jane
Where do you live?
Down the grid.
What number?
Cucumber.
What street?
Pig street.

Write down any rhyme of this kind which you know, and add it to the name rhymes you have already collected if you or another group in the class have done the tasks on page 12.

SURNAMES

Before the Middle Ages ordinary people did not need a surname. Most peasants lived on small farms or in villages where everyone knew everyone else, and since people did not move far from the place they were born in, no-one needed surnames. As the population increased and people began to move about it was no longer enough to know that a person was John or Mary, you had to know which one of several Johns or Marys. The surnames which came into use at this time can be divided into four main groups:

1 those which tell us where a person lived
2 those which tell us what he looked like
3 those which tell us who his father was, and
4 those which tell us what job he did.

Some of the names based on places are easy to spot: a person called York or London came from that place. Newcomers to England might be named after the country they came from, e.g. French, Scott, Welch (Welsh) or Pollack (Polish). More often men were named after a village landmark near which they lived; someone living near the village green might be given the surname Green, or the person living near the bridge might become known as Brigg.

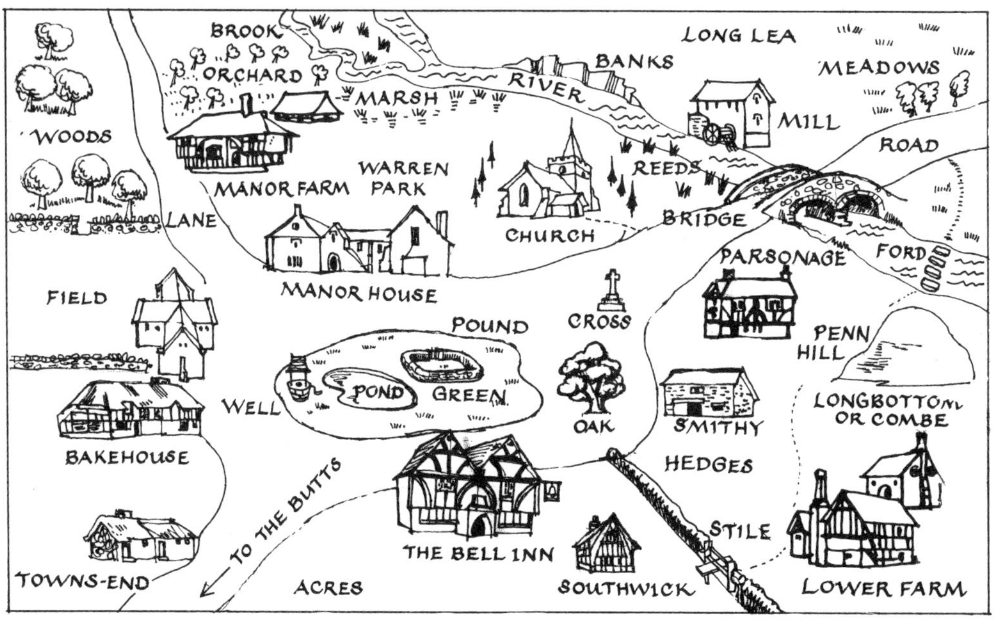

Look at the map opposite which shows an imaginary Medieval village. Write down as many origins for surnames as you can from the places marked on the map.

Some of the names based on what a person looked like are straightforward physical descriptions such as Large, Strong or Short. Other names need a bit more thought: Black means dark-haired and White fair-haired. We all know sayings which compare human beings to animals, such as 'quiet as a mouse' or 'meek as a lamb'. Resemblances between people and animals were often used for surnames – and not always in a complimentary way. We can guess from their names something about the people who were first called Bull, Hogg (pig), Fox or Lamb. Other names were very uncomplimentary for example, Milksopp or Sheepshank (shank means leg). Sometimes nicknames stuck and became permanent surnames such as Dolittle, Gotobed or Makepeace.

Other surnames arose when people were known by who their father was; so John Peter's son became John Peterson. There are many other surnames which were formed like this such as Johnson, Adamson and Davi(d)son. Sometimes the 'son' was shortened simply to 's' and so we get Peters, Johns, Davis, Harris (Harry's son) or Dickens (Dick's son). This same pattern of naming is found in Scotland where instead of 'son' at the end of a name you get 'Mac' at the beginning; so MacDonald means 'son of Donald' and so on. In Ireland the 'O' at the front of a name (being short for 'of') means the same thing and this gives us names like O'Henry, O'Neil, O'Riley and O'Brian. The Welsh form of this same thing is 'Ap', but this is more often shortened to just a 'P' at the beginning, for example Prichard for 'son of Richard' and Parry for 'son of Harry'. A few surnames of this kind come from the mother's name, such as Margerison (son of Margery) and Margotson (son of Margaret).

Probably the biggest group of surnames are those which tell us about the job a person did. Some are so obvious that they don't need further explanation, even though the occupations themselves may now be rare, for example, Thatcher, Miller, Archer, Cobbler or Shepherd. You should be able to think of plenty more of these for yourself. To explain some of the other names in this group we need to go back to Medieval occupations: a Fletcher was someone who made arrows, a Cooper was a barrel maker; wright meant a person who made things so a Wheelwright made wheels and a Wainwright made wains (or hay waggons). The lord of a Medieval manor employed many people in his household and on his estate: in the house he would need a Cook, a Butler (to look after his wine) and perhaps if he were very rich even a Merryman (or jester) to entertain him. He would need a Steward (later also spelled Stewart) to look after his estates, a Forester (also later Forster and Foster) to look after the woods in which he hunted game, a Falconer (Faulkner) for his falcons and hawks, a Warrener (Warner, Warren) for the rabbit warrens which provided food for the people on the estate, and many more.

In the Middle Ages people often used to go on pilgrimages or journeys to special holy places; someone who had done this might be given the name Pilgrim. A pilgrim who had been all the way to the Holy Land would carry a palm leaf to show this and might be called Palmer. Because most people could not read, plays known as Mystery plays which told stories from the Bible were performed on special days. Parts in these plays were often passed down from father to son and so a man might be known by the part he played. This gave rise to surnames such as King, Prince, Bishop, Pope or Knight.

When the Normans, led by William the Conqueror, invaded England they brought with them many French names; often these were the names of places they came from. Other names which are French in origin were changed or pronounced wrongly by the English to give us names which now don't sound French at all; for example Mullins which comes from 'moulin' meaning a mill.

Many parts of the country have their own characteristic surnames and you can often have a good guess at where a person's family originated from their surname. It is easy to see that a name beginning with 'Mac' comes from Scotland but there are other names, such as Stuart or Hamilton which are also Scottish. In Wales we find that many people share surnames such as Davies, Williams, Jones, Thomas or Evans. There is an old rhyme about Cornish names:

By Tre-, Gar-, Pol- and Pen-
Shall ye know Cornish men.

If we look at Cornish names we can find many which follow the rhyme such as Trevithick, Trethowan, Poldark, Penrose and Pentreath.

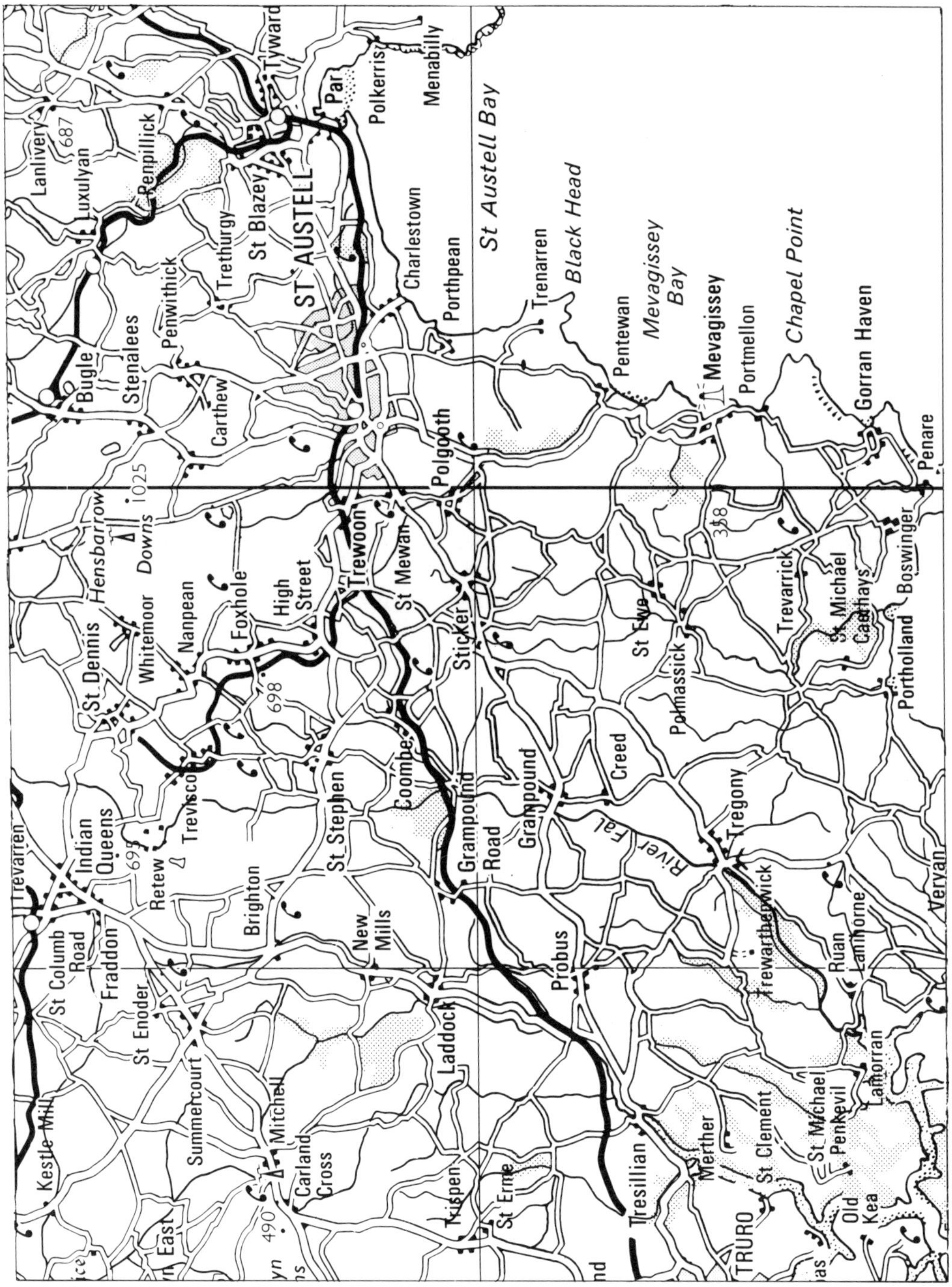

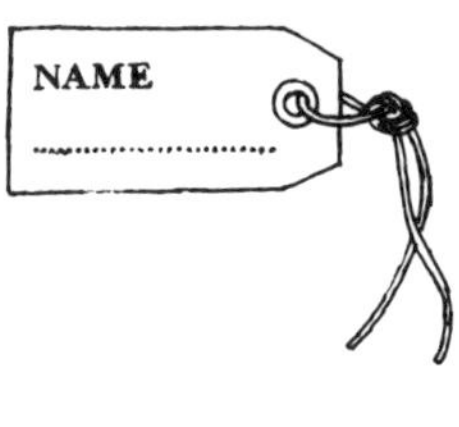

Look at the section from the Ordnance Survey map for part of Cornwall shown above. You will see that the place names also follow the same pattern as the surnames. Make a list of as many places on the map as you can find to fit each of the four beginnings.

Many surnames which come from Yorkshire are names of places there, such as Kirby or Ramsbottom; other names contain the same northern or Viking words for parts of the land as are found in the place names; for example thwaite (clearing) as in Postlethwaite or Braithwaite; Scarr and Scargill from scarr which means valley (gill is a deep valley).

Find out the origin of your own surname; you will need to use some reference books for this. When the whole class has done this you can put the results together.

Either set your results out as a chart showing the four kinds of origin for surnames and listing them so that all the names from jobs are in one column, all the names from where a person lived in another column and so on.

Or you could arrange the names according to which part of the country they come from.

If you live in a small community you can find out which surnames were most common in your area by going to look at the gravestones in your local churchyard.

Make a list of the surnames you find and note how often you find each one.

Do you know people in the area who still have those names? You can check if the same names are still found often in your area by checking the number of entries for each one in the local telephone directory.

If you live in a city or an area which people move in and out of a lot you may not be able to do this. Instead you can make a list of the names which appear most often in your telephone directory; from this, you can work out the areas of the British Isles or of the world from which people have moved into your area.

Signs for names

Medieval Knights began to need coats of arms so that they could be recognised easily when they were wearing armour. They often had pictures on their arms which were connected with their names or were a kind of joke about their name. The Lucy family chose as their sign a pike (fish) because 'luce' was an old word for pike.

Look at the coats of arms shown on this page. When you have found out the meaning or origin of your own name, see if you can think of a suitable design for your coat of arms. You should base your coat of arms on the meaning of your name, or you could make a pun or joke about it.

If you have some books on heraldry in your school library, you can check up on how to divide up the shield and what colours to use.

NICKNAMES

Most of us have a nickname at some time in our lives – usually when we are at school. Children like making up funny (and sometimes unkind!) names for each other. These are often to do with what a person looks like such as 'Fatty', 'Piggy', 'Tank', 'Tich', 'Shorty' or 'Lanky'. Some nicknames are used so often that there are rhymes about them.

Sometimes nicknames are based on a person's real name, such as 'Ding Dong' for someone called 'Bell'. Other names have nicknames which always go with them like 'Nobby' Clark or 'Dusty' Miller. People's characters are often used in their nicknames, for example 'Scrooge' for someone mean or 'Professor' for someone brainy.

Make a list of the nicknames people in your class use or have used. Beside each one write, if you can, how each one started.

Write down any rhymes you know about particular nicknames. Collect them together from all the class and put them together with your name rhymes.

School subjects often have nicknames. Chemistry is often known as 'Stinks' (and the Chemistry teacher as 'Sir Stinks'), and French as 'Froggy Lingo'.

Turkish surnames

Until about 45 years ago people in Turkey did not have surnames. This caused a lot of confusion. The husband in each family was asked to choose a surname for himself and his children. Most of them chose names which were descriptions of themselves as they were (or would have liked to be!) such as Mr Polite, Mr Well-Behaved, or Mr Mad-Smoke and Mr Cartridge. Other names were less flattering, for example Mr Swollen-Leg or Mr Dwarfman-of-Iron.

Try to think up surnames for yourself and your friends which might fit you, perhaps better than the names you were born with. In turn, read out one of your invented surnames and see if the rest of the class can guess who you mean.

WHAT'S FOR DINNER?

School dinners have a class of names all their own!

Splishy splashy custard,
Dead dogs' eyes,
All mixed up with giblet pies,
Spread it on the butty nice and thick,
Wash it all down with a cup of cold sick.

Can you guess what's for dinner at this school?
(Answers on page 48.)

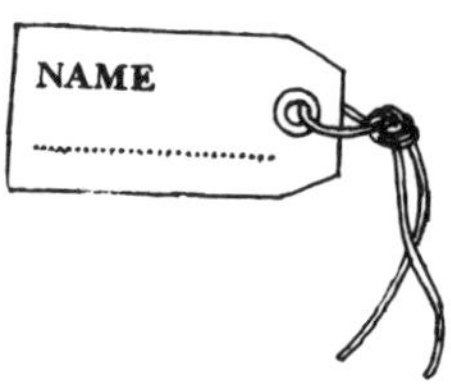

In a group, collect together all the names you have for school dinners. You can make your own *Dictionary of School Food*.

Tom Tit Tot

This story is found in different forms all over Europe. You will probably find that you remember it (from when you were younger) under a different name. As you read through it, look out for any bits that are different from the story you know and make a note of them.

There was once a woman who baked five pies for dinner, and she left them in the oven too long. They were cooked quite hard, so that the knife would not cut them. She put them away on the shelf, saying they would come again. By this she meant that they would get soft, and could be eaten later. But her daughter Joan overheard her, and said to herself:

'Why, if they will come again, I may as well eat them.'

So being hungry she ate all the five pies, hard as they were, and very good she found them.

When supper-time came her mother said:

'Joan, go and fetch two or three of those pies.'

Joan went to the larder and looked on the shelf, but of course they were not there.

'They haven't come again yet,' said she to her mother, 'so you can't have them.'

'Not come yet?' said her mother. 'Fetch one of them, and let's have a look.'

'I can't fetch one,' said Joan, 'for not even one of them has come again. I ate them all, and I ought to know.'

'You've eaten all the five pies?' asked her mother in surprise. 'What a wonderful fine appetite you have, to be sure.'

As there were no pies for supper, she went and sat in the doorway and began spinning. And as she spun, she sang to herself, and this is what she sang:

'My daughter has eaten five –
Five pies today.'

Now it happened that the King was passing down the street at that moment, and he heard the woman singing, so he said:

'What song is that you are singing, ma'am?'

The woman did not like to tell the King the real

words, because she did not want him to think her daughter was greedy, so she changed the words.

'"My daughter has spun five – five skeins today." Those are the words I was singing, Your Majesty.'

With that the woman rose from her stool and made the King a curtsy.

'Indeed?' said the King. 'What a wonderful spinner your daughter is! I should like to see her.'

The woman brought out her daughter, and the King said:

'It happens that I am looking for a wife. You seem a likely girl, as well as a wonderful spinner. How would you like to marry me and be Queen?'

'I should like it very much, Your Majesty,' said Joan, and made a deep curtsy.

'Very well,' said the King. 'I will marry you, and for eleven months of the year you may have fine clothes and all the money you want, all the food you need, and whatever company you like. But for the twelfth month of the year you must spin me five skeins of flaxen thread every day. What do you say?'

Now Joan and her mother knew very well that she could never spin five skeins a day, for that is a very great deal, even for a practised spinner; but they thought that when the time came, some way out of the difficulty could be found. So they told the King they were willing for him to marry Joan on those conditions.

Joan and the King were married, and there was a magnificent ceremony, and for the first few months everything went well. Joan had all the food she wanted, money and fine clothes, and whatever company she liked; though the company she liked best was that of the King himself, for as the months went on, she loved him more and more dearly. The eleven months went all too quickly, but Joan hoped that the King had forgotten all about the five skeins a day she had promised to spin during the last month. However, when the last day of the eleventh month came, he took her up to a room at the top of the castle, where she had never been before. In it there was nothing but a spinning-wheel, a stool, a bare table, and a bed for her to lie on.

'This is where you must stay for a whole month,' he said. 'Every morning I shall bring you your breakfast and the flax to spin, and every evening I shall bring you your supper and take away the five skeins of yarn you have spun during the day. But the very first time you fail to spin the five skeins, next day your head will be cut off.'

As soon as poor Joan was left to herself, she sat down on the stool and began to cry. However was she to spin *one* skein of flax in a day, let alone five? She was a clumsy girl with her hands, and had never learnt to use a spinning-wheel. The King would bring her the flax and return for the skeins of yarn in the evening, and he would discover she was no spinner at all, so her head would be cut off, and that would be the end of her marriage and her life as well.

Then as she sat crying, Joan heard a little sound of knocking at the door, and she said, 'Come in,' and into the room came a small black thing with very bright

eyes, twitching pointed ears, and a long tail. He looked at Joan out of the corners of his eyes and said:

'What's the matter here?'

'That's nothing to you,' answered Joan.

'Maybe it is, and maybe it isn't,' That said. 'Tell me what it is, and I shall know.'

So Joan told him all about the burnt pies and her marriage to the King and the five skeins of flax that she had to spin or have her head cut off.

'Well, I can help you,' That said. 'Every morning when you get the flax, I will come along and take it away with me, and in the evening I will bring it back, spun into five skeins.'

'I see,' said Joan, 'and what is your price?'

'Every day I will give you three guesses,' said the little black thing, 'and you just guess my name. If you don't guess it by the time the month is up, I shall have you for myself.'

'All right,' said Joan, 'it's a bargain.'

What else could she do? She knew she could never spin the flax herself, and if nobody helped her, she would certainly lose her head. Besides, she was sure she could think of the name of the little black thing before the end of the month. Without further words, That twirled That's tail, rose up in the air, and flew out of the window.

Next morning the King brought Joan her breakfast and the flax to spin and left her to herself. No sooner had he gone than That came flying in and took away the flax. So Joan spent the day thinking of names that That might be called.

Just as darkness was falling, in flew the black thing with the five skeins of flax, and very skilfully they had been spun.

'Now,' said he, 'what's my name? You have three guesses.'

'Might it be Bill?' said Joan.

That twirled That's tail and said: 'No, it mightn't.'

'Might it be Ned?' asked Joan.

That laughed.

'No,' That said. 'It might not neither.'

'Then maybe it is Mark,' said Joan.

That twirled That's tail and laughed again.

'That it might not,' That said, and flew off out of the window.

Presently the King came in with some supper, and he was mighty pleased when he saw the five skeins of flax.

'Well, my dear,' he said, 'you won't have to be beheaded tomorrow, I see.'

Next day the King brought more flax, and That came and took it away and brought it back in the evening and asked Joan what his name was. Every day the same thing happened, but still Joan could not guess his name. She tried everything she knew – names of the boys she had known at home, names from story-books, and names from the Bible. And the nearer and nearer came the end of the month, the more gleeful and malicious That grew, twirling his tail and rolling his little fiery eyes.

On the last day but one he brought the finished skeins as usual, and as usual he said, 'What's my name?'

'Happen it's Nicodemus,' said Joan.

'Happen it's not then,' said the little imp, laughing spitefully. 'What next?'

'Then maybe it's Sammle,' said Joan.

'And maybe it isn't,' said the imp, twirling his tail fiercely.

'Then it must be Methusalem,' said Joan, almost in despair.

'That it's not,' said he with a terrible laugh. 'There's only one more day, my girl, and you shall be mine!'

And That twirled That's tail so maliciously that it could scarce be seen, and glared at Joan out of his fiery eyes till she felt terribly frightened. Then off he flew.

Poor Joan was in a bad way, but the King, when he came in with supper and the last of the flax, looked more pleased than ever.

'I don't doubt, my dear,' he said, 'that you'll spin the five skeins tomorrow just as you have spun them every day before; so to show how happy I am that your life will be spared, I have brought my own supper and will sit and eat it with you.'

Never a word said Joan about the little black imp, and together they ate their supper. Hardly had the King eaten a mouthful when he burst out laughing.

'What is there to be so happy about?' asked Joan.

'Why, my dear,' answered the King, 'I almost forgot

to tell you. The funniest thing happened today when I was out hunting. We got to the edge of a wood, and down at the bottom of an old chalk-pit was sitting a little black creature with a twirling tail. He was sitting on a stool spinning away at a small spinning-wheel. It was turning away as fast as fast, and as it turned the black creature sang. This is what it sang, and I can't make head nor tail of it.

"Nimmy nimmy not –
My name is TOM TIT TOT!"
Now what do you make of that, my dear?'

Joan's heart was leaping for joy, but she said nothing. When the King had gone, she repeated the rhyme to herself over and over again to make sure she remembered it right, and after that she fell asleep.

Next evening That brought back the finished skeins just as before, and this time he was looking more crafty and gleeful than ever. He gave her the skeins and asked:

'What is my name?'

Joan pretended to be frightened.

'Might it be – Solomon?' she asked.

'Try again!' shouted the imp, grinning horribly, and coming farther into the room.

Joan hesitated, and paused as if she were thinking desperately.

'Then it must be Zebedee,' she said faintly.

'Not that neither!' shouted the imp with a devilish laugh, coming still closer to Joan and holding out his little black hands towards her. 'One more guess, my little one, and then you are mine!'

Joan shrank back into a corner of the room as if she were dreadfully frightened, and at last she pointed a finger at the little black demon, and said with a joyful laugh:

'Nimmy nimmy not –
Your name is TOM TIT TOT!'

Instantly there was a flash of lightning, a clap of thunder; Tom Tit Tot gave a great cry, twirled his tail in spite and anger, and flew out of the window, his eyes blazing like coals of fire. And that was the end of That – for Joan never saw him again. When the King came in, he brought Joan no supper – instead, he took one look at the five finished skeins, and led Joan downstairs to feast with him in his own hall.

In a group, look through the points you jotted down as you were reading through the story – what did you call it? which details were different from the story you knew? how important were the differences?

You can act out this story. You will need a narrator to read the linking bits, the girl, her mother, the King and Tom Tit Tot. As the narrator is reading the actors will need to act out the parts of the story he is describing. You may want to cut some bits out to shorten the narrator's part.

This story would make a good puppet play. You could use the story as explained above, or you could use it as the basis for writing your own script.

If you have, or can improvise, a puppet theatre you will also need someone to paint backdrops for each of the three scenes – in the street, in the room and in the wood. Someone else will be needed, to make the props such as the pies and the spinning wheel.

For the puppets themselves, glove puppets would be the easiest.

Make the head first using papier mache. To get the basic shape you can use a ball of plasticine; when you have built up the first three or four layers of papier mache and they are dry, cut through them and remove the plasticine. Put the two hollow halves together again and add another layer of paper all over, this will hold them together. The shape of the face can then be built up using more paper. When it is all dry you can paint it.

A tube of cardboard forms the neck to which the head and clothing are attached and inside which your first finger fits when working the puppet.

When you have made the basic fabric body to fit your hand, you can add suitable trimmings for the character you are making, such as a crown for the King.

When you perform the play, if you want to include more people, you can have different people working the puppets and doing the voices.

PLACE NAMES

The picture above shows the station sign from the place in Britain which has the longest name. This is in Anglesey in Wales. Have a go at reading it out loud! (The 'Ll-' is pronounced 'Cl-'). The other places shown on this page have names which are easier to say, but are just as interesting. It is easy to see where a name like Blackpool or Cambridge comes from; we may have to think harder or do some investigation to find the meanings of other place names.

The first people to settle in Britain were mostly farmers and they often named places after local landmarks. They picked out the things which were important to them such as rivers, hills and fields, or named places after the people who lived there. With a little practice you can soon learn to identify the different parts of place names and what they mean.

Sometimes there are different words in different parts of the country for the same thing, so a name may also help you to guess whereabouts in the country the place is. The Old English word for a valley is 'dene', this gives us villages called Dean or Deane; it can also appear as '-den' on the end of a name, such as Haslingden (valley of hazels). The Danes called a valley 'dale' so in Yorkshire, where many Vikings settled, there are lots of names with 'dale' in them –

Nidderdale (valley of the river Nidd), Wensleydale (valley by Wendel's wood). The Gaelic word for valley is 'cwm'; this was the same as 'combe' in Old English. There are several places in Britain called Combe or Coombe, and many places which have '-combe' or 'Com-' as part of them. For example Withycombe, which means valley full of willows (withy is an old word for a willow tree) and Ilfracombe, which means 'valley of Alfred's people'. Many places in Wales have 'cwm' as part of them.

Because most of the early settlers were farmers many of the place names they gave have 'field' in them, so Stanfield was a 'stony field'. Trees were also important to them and the Old English word for a wood gives us 'leigh' (also spelt 'ley' or 'leah') which is found as part of many place names. They often had to clear away trees to make their fields. The names they left behind give us a clue as to what trees they were – Oakley and Ashley are clear enough; there was a birch wood at Berkeley and brooms at Bramley.

If you look at the map on the following two pages you will see some of the commonest parts of British place names, what they mean and where they are found most.

British place names

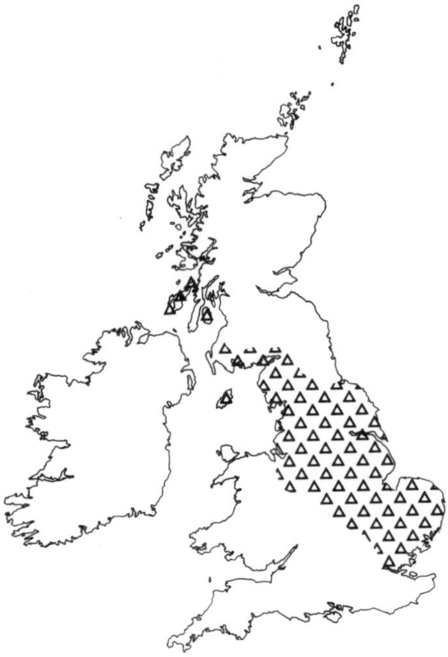

VIKING

-by: farm or village, as in Derby, Denby, Normanby, Selby and Welby

-thwaite: clearing or meadow, (usually found in Yorkshire and the Lake District) as in Braithwaite, Applethwaite and Krikthwaite

-thorpe: settlement or hamlet, as found in Alethorpe, Grassthorpe and Hackthorpe

ANGLO-SAXON

-ham: homestead or estate (modern home) as in Fordham, Grantham, Horsham and Wickham

-ing: from 'ingas', a group of people, as in Hastings, Reading, Terling and Tooting.

-ingham: a mixture of 'ingas' and 'ham' as found in Birmingham, Nottingham and Walsingham

-tun/ton: enclosure, village or farm (modern home) as in Skipton, Frampton, Nuneaton and Everton

-ington: a mixture of 'ingas' and 'tun' as found in Rushington, Washington and Donington

-ford: a place where the river could be crossed as in Appleford, Oxford, Stratford and Stanford

-burgh/bury: fortified place as found in Edinburgh, Bury, Sedburgh and Whittlebury

-cester, -chester, -caster: Roman town or fort as in Chester, Manchester, Cirencester and Lancaster

-stow: a holy place as found in Padstow, Walthamstow, Stowe and Felixstowe

-dun/don: hill as in Maldon, Lyndon, Clevedon, Dunham and Dunning

CELTIC

baile: farm or homestead (found mostly in Scotland and Ireland), as in Ballachulish, Ballater and Ballyquirk

avon: river, as in Avonmouth, Avonbridge and Avonwick. There are no less than nine rivers called the Avon in Britain – can you find them all?

burn/bourne: stream, as in Sittingbourne, Blackburn, Lambourn and Kilburn

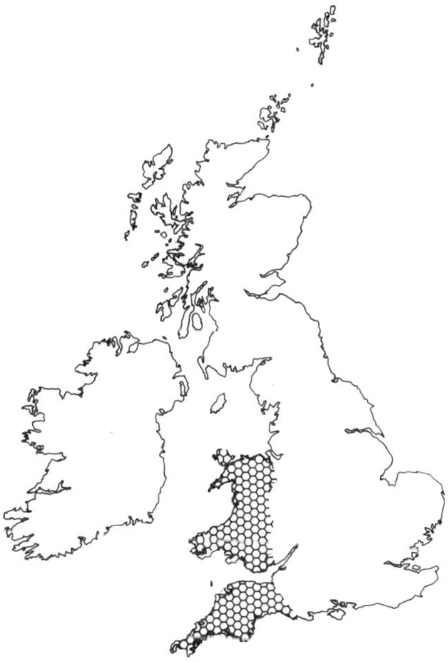

NORMAN

By the time the Normans came most places already had Anglo-Saxon names, so they tended to add French bits to existing names for example: Ashby de le Zouche, Chapel en le Frith, Preston Bissett and Stoke Poges.

Some places have names which are entirely French, usually when the landowner gave a new name to his manor as in Beaulieu or Herstmonceux.

WELSH/CORNISH

caer: fortress, as in Caernarvon, Caerleon, Caerphilly and Caerwent

tre: farmstead, as in Tregarth, Trefilan and Tremaine

aber: mouth of a river, as in Abergavenny, Aberdeen, Aberdovey and Aberystwyth

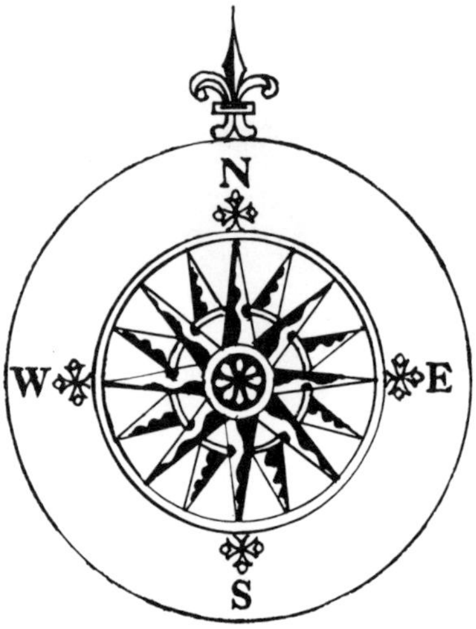

North-tun
Norton
Norbury
Norleigh

West-tun
Weston
Western
Westley
Westbury
(Wessex)

Middle-tun
Middleton
Milton
(Middlesex)

East-tun
Easton
Aston
Eastleigh
(Essex)

South-tun
Sutton
Sudley
Sudbury
(Sussex)

As you can see from the information on the previous pages, names are often made up of several parts, each of which tells us something about the place and its origin. Sometimes a part of the name is a compass direction, particularly where there are several villages close together with the same name; another way of distinguishing two places with the same name is to call them Upper and Lower, as is found in Upper Slaughter and Lower Slaughter in Gloucestershire (the second part of the name is not as grim as it sounds, Slaughter comes from two Old English words meaning 'muddy place'). A big county like Yorkshire was also divided into North, West and East Ridings (Riding comes from the Old English thirding meaning a third). Perhaps the relationship between the old Saxon counties is not so obvious – Sussex means land of the South Saxons, so you should be able to work out what Essex, Wessex and Middlesex mean.

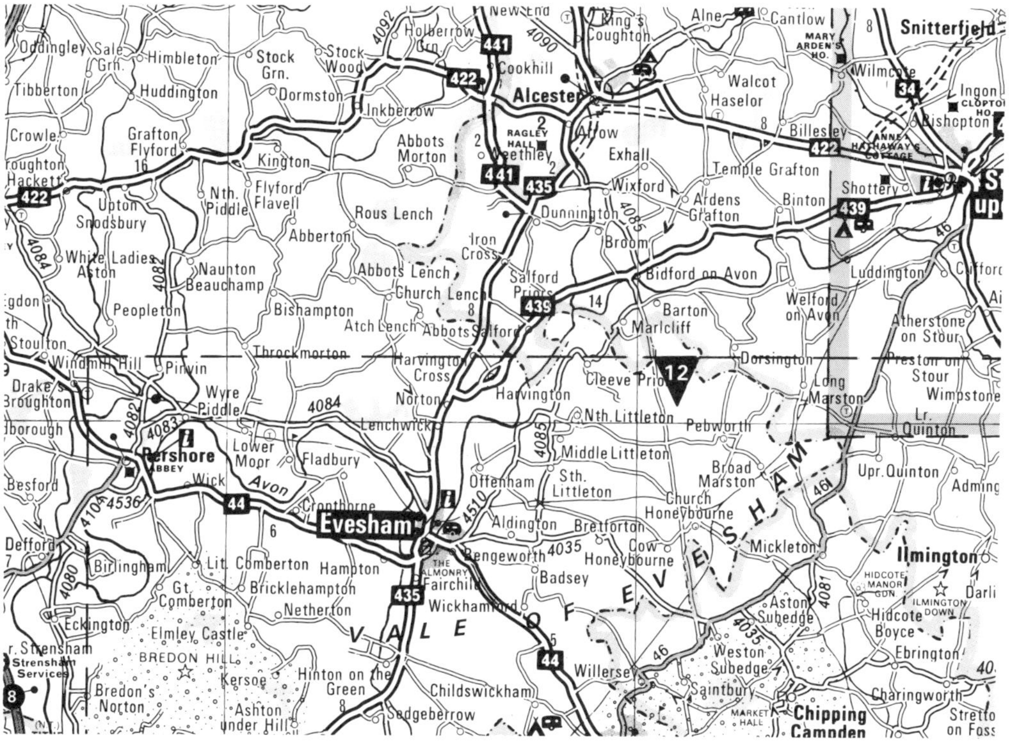

The map at the top of the opposite page shows the area of the country around Evesham and Stratford-upon-Avon. If you look carefully at the map you will see that there are several groups of villages which have the same name.

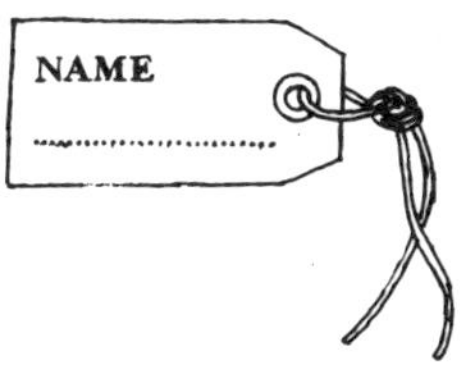

Can you find the three Littletons? How are they distinguished?

There are two villages called Quinton (Queen's farm) – can you find their names?

There are also two Marstons (marsh farm) and two Subedges (at the foot of a ridge or edge), can you find these pairs and see how they are differentiated?

When the people of Britain became converted to Christianity this was reflected in the names of places around the country. It is easy to see how a village where a church was built might get 'Church' added to its name (Church Stretton, Church Hanborough, Church Leigh). A place might be named after a saint, especially if he or she was a local figure (St Albans, St Ives, St Kilda, St Mawes). When the Church grew powerful and began to own land, a village might have the owner's name added to its own; so we find Abbotts Bromley, Bishops Sutton or Preston (priest's farm).

On the map (p. 37) are four villages called Lench. Can you find them and see which ones have a connection with the church? (Rous = Ralph's, Atch = Aetti's?).

One of the Honeybournes (Huna's stream) has a religious connection. What do you think the other one was connected with?

Several of the villages are named after the stream or river by which they are built. If you follow the course of the rivers Stour and Avon on the map you should be able to find several examples of this.

You can also find many more interesting names on the map (e.g. White Ladies Aston or Upton Snodbury); if you are interested you can try looking up the meanings of some of these.

You will need a road map or an Ordnance Survey map of your own local area to investigate the names in your part of the country. Check with the information on pages 34–35 and then try to arrange the names in groups according to whether they are Celtic, Old English (Anglo-Saxon) etc., in origin.

Are there any with the ending '-cester' or '-caster'? If so, are there any other signs on your map of the Roman occupation?

Look out for groups of villages such as those we found on the Evesham map.

Can you find names which tell you about the land e.g. names with 'hill', 'ford', 'leigh', 'wood' etc., in them?

Make a list of any names which seem unusual or might be foreign in origin, and then try to find out their meanings.

Street names can often tell us about the history of the town or village in which we live. Sometimes a street may simply be named from its position, such as North Street or South Side; or the name may refer to a local feature, for example Church Lane or Town Hall Square. Streets are often named as a tribute to famous people or to commemorate events at the time when the houses were built; the origin of Trafalgar Square should be obvious, though for Jubilee Terrace or Coronation Street we may need to find out which coronation or jubilee it refers to.

The origins of some names are not so obvious and may need some investigation to track down – Nizewell Head, for example, comes from Nine Wells Head and refers to the favoured position people who lived there were in during the days before everyone had piped water.

When a new estate is built the names of the roads often follow a theme; so, for example, they may all be kinds of trees, or famous writers, or names of places in a certain area of the country like the Lake District or the Yorkshire Dales.

Present names may refer to a previous use for the street – the origin of Horsefair in Birmingham should be obvious, and Sheep Street in Bicester used to be the scene of the local sheep market.

How do you think the following streets got their names:

Cattlemarket St in Norwich
Fuller's Row in Swansea
Tithebarn St in Liverpool
Saltmarket in Glasgow
Petticoat Lane and Threadneedle Street in London?

(You may need to look up what a fuller did and what tithes were.)

If you look at the street name-plates at the top of the page, you will see that they are written in a variety of different kinds of lettering.

A group of you could make a display of rubbings of street names in your area. Try to get as many different lettering styles as you can to make it more interesting.

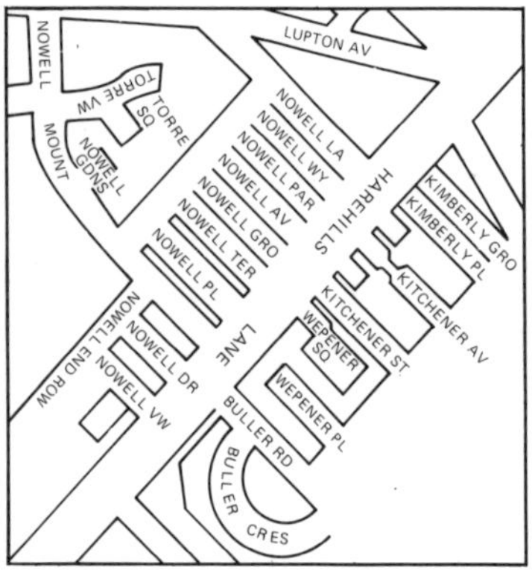

As you can see from the examples on the previous page, there are many different words for street.

Make a list of as many of these words as you can think of, and beside each one write what you think the name tells you about the road. For example:

a Crescent is a road built in a curve
a Terrace is a row of houses joined together
an Avenue always used to be a road with trees down each side.

It may help you to look at the section of the map of Leeds shown alongside.

Look carefully at the street map opposite, which shows the centre of Durham. You can see where the remains of Durham Castle are and also the line of the old city walls (marked by the dotted lines). If you look at the names of the streets you will find the history of the city recorded in them. North Bailey and South Bailey go back to the time when the castle was the most important part of Durham – a bailey was a defensive wall to a castle. What do you think Moatside Lane refers to?

Several of the street names have '-gate' in them. This dates back to medieval times when the city had a wall round it and the only way in or out of the city was through one of the gates in the wall.

Some of the names go back to the time when the people doing the same job would live in the same street. What do you think you would have gone to buy in Bakehouse Lane, Sadler Street and Silver Street?

Other names describe the area around. What do you think it was like by Claypath, or Briardene (dene = valley)? Where would you expect to find Waterside? Some names tell us about the use men have made of the land. What do you think was done at Archery Rise, Quarryheads Lane or Anchorage Terrace?

Some places are named after people. Why is it likely that Gladstone Villas, Albert Street and Alexandra Crescent were all given their names in Queen Victoria's time?

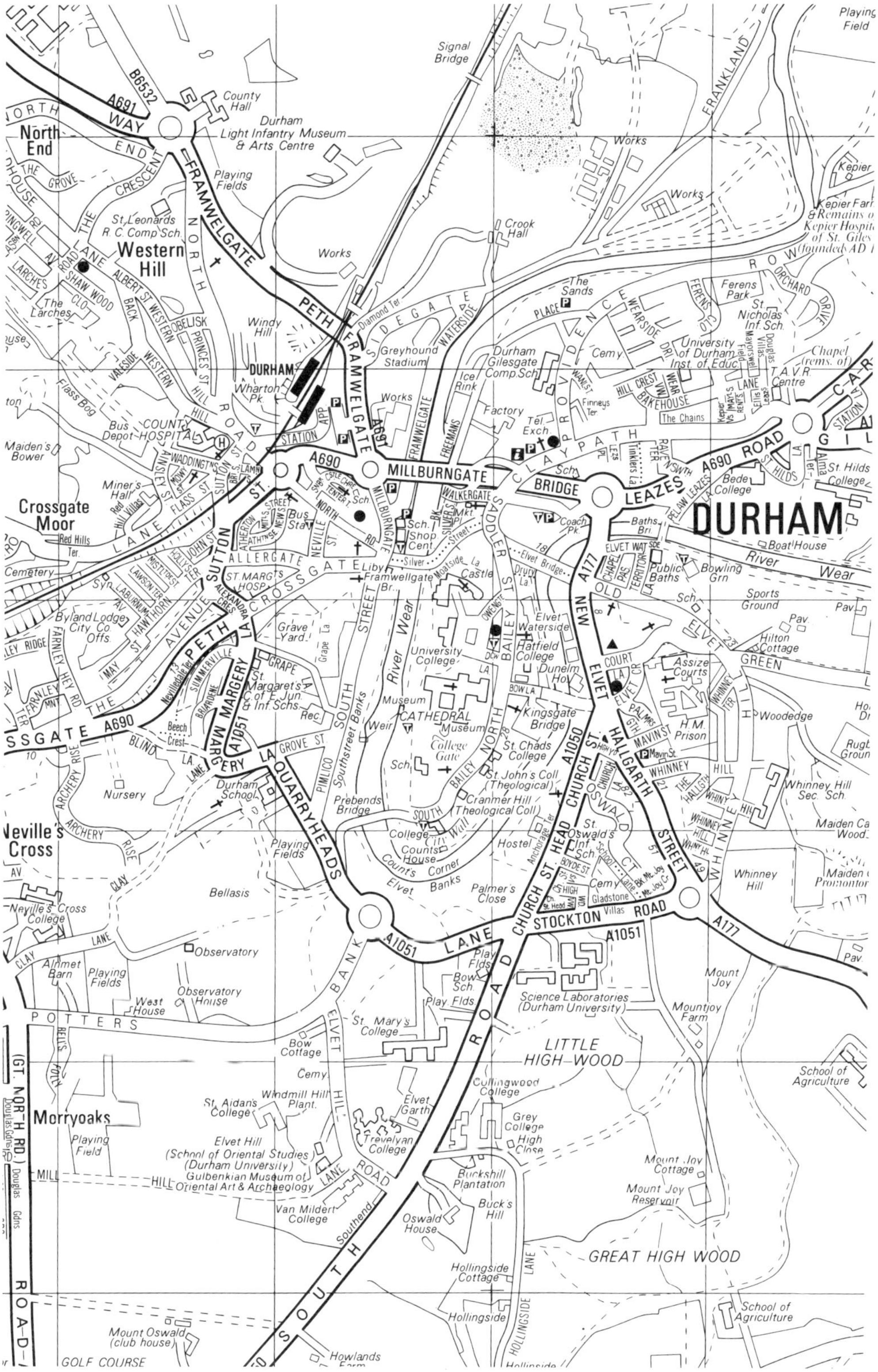
DURHAM
North End
Western Hill
Crossgate Moor
Neville's Cross
Morryoaks
County Hall
Durham Light Infantry Museum & Arts Centre
Playing Fields
St. Leonards R.C. Comp Sch.
Signal Bridge
Crook Hall
Works
Windy Hill
Wharton Pk.
Greyhound Stadium
Durham Gilesgate Comp.Sch.
Ice Rink
Factory
Tel. Exch.
The Sands
Ferens Park
St. Nicholas Inf.Sch.
University of Durham Inst. of Educ.
T.A.V.R. Centre
Kepier Farm & Remains of Kepier Hospital of St. Giles
Bede College
St. Hilds College
Boat House
River Wear
Bowling Grn
Sports Ground
Public Baths
Hilton Cottage
Assize Courts
H.M. Prison
Woodedge
Whinney Hill Sec. Sch.
Whinney Hill
COUNTY HOSPITAL
Bus Depot
Maiden's Bower
Miner's Hall
Flass Bog
Cemetery
Byland Lodge City Co. Offs.
ST.MARG'TS HOSP.
Grave Yard
St. Margaret's C of E Jun. & Inf. Schs.
Castle
University College
CATHEDRAL
Museum
College Gate
Hatfield College
Dunelm Hoy
Elvet Waterside
Kingsgate Bridge
St. Chads College
St. John's Coll (Theological)
Cranmer Hill (Theological Coll)
St. Oswald's Inf. Sch.
Cemy
Hostel
Palmer's Close
Elvet Banks
Count's Corner
Counts House
Prebends Bridge
Southstreet Banks
Durham School
Nursery
Bellasis
Observatory
Observatory House
West House
Neville's Cross College
Almet Barn
Playing Fields
Play Flds
Bow Sch.
Science Laboratories (Durham University)
LITTLE HIGH WOOD
Mount Joy
Mountjoy Farm
School of Agriculture
St. Mary's College
Bow Cottage
Cemy.
St. Aidan's College
Windmill Hill Plant.
Elvet Garth
Trevelyan College
Elvet Hill (School of Oriental Studies) (Durham University)
Gulbenkian Museum of Oriental Art & Archaeology
Van Mildert College
Collingwood College
Grey College
High Close
Buckshill Plantation
Buck's Hill
Oswald House
Mount Joy Cottage
Mount Joy Reservoir
GREAT HIGH WOOD
Hollingside Cottage
Hollingside
Mount Oswald (club house)
GOLF COURSE
Howlands Farm
A691 NORTH WAY
B6532
FRAMWELGATE PETH
NORTH ROAD
A690 MILLBURNGATE BRIDGE
CLAYPATH
LEAZES A690 ROAD
GILESGATE
NEW ELVET A177
SADDLER ST.
SILVER ST.
SOUTH STREET
CROSSGATE
ALLERGATE
SUTTON ST.
CROSSGATE A690 PETH
MARGERY LA A1051
QUARRYHEADS
A1051 STOCKTON ROAD
CHURCH ST. A1050
HALLGARTH STREET
SOUTH ROAD
ELVET HILL ROAD
POTTERS BANK
MILL HILL LANE
HOLLINGSIDE LANE
(GT. NORTH RD.) ROAD
ELVET GREEN
OLD ELVET
WHINNEY HILL
PROVIDENCE ROW
FRANKLAND
SIDEGATE
FRAMWELGATE WATERSIDE
ARCHERY RISE
CLAY LANE
BLIND LANE
GROVE ST.
GRAPE LANE

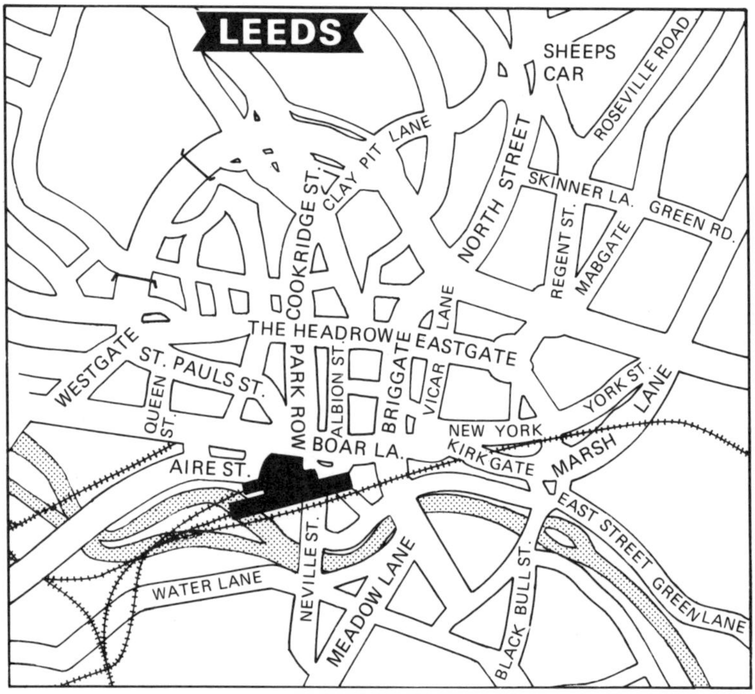

Look carefully at the street map above which shows part of Leeds city centre.

How many street names can you find which tell you that they used to lead to gates in the old city wall?

What else do the names Briggate and Kirkgate tell you? (Kirk is a northern/older word meaning church).

How many street names can you find which refer to kings and queens?

Can you find any names which tell you what the area is like, or what that part of the town was used for?

Which streets are named after places in London?

A group of you can work together to draw a large-scale map of the streets near where you live. Label them clearly and find out the origins of as many of the names as you can. (You may need to look at books on the local history of your area to follow up some of the names.)

You can then make your map into a wall display or a booklet. If you have a camera available, you could illustrate it with photographs.

HOUSE NAMES

People often like to give their house a name. In a village there may be no numbers and so houses are identified by name. On an estate owners may wish to make their home different from all the other houses which look like it.

A house may be called after a place the owners have visited, or its name may be based on the names of the inhabitants. Sometimes the name may comment on the position in which the house stands, such as Windy Ridge, or its history, as in Saddler's Cottage or Pound House (where the village pound used to be). Often house names are jokey such as Fool's Haven, Popinagen or Ourome; sometimes it is hard to work out what a house name means, what do you make of Barbrob for example? One house was given the name Luncheons because the new owners found a sign in the cellar left by the previous owners, so what had been an advertisement turned into a name. Cobwebs sounds a romantic name for a house but the owners said they called it that because it was **C**urrently **O**wned **B**y **W**oolwich **E**quitable **B**uilding **S**ociety who had loaned them the money to buy it!

Names are also given to boats and caravans, and people often give a freer rein to their imagination or their sense of humour than they would when naming their more permanent homes. Houseboats in particular seem to be given long names which go from the sublime to the ridiculous e.g. Brain of Pooh or Isambard Kingdom Brunel, which can be seen moored side by side on the Oxford Canal.

A group of you can collect house names which people in your class know of. Find out if the owners gave their houses that name and if they did, ask them how the name originated.

Another group of you can collect names of houses in the area around your school. It makes it more interesting if you can guess at, or find out, how the names came into being.

NAMES FOR PUBS

Every town and village in the country has its pub or pubs and their names and signs make an interesting study. Inns are often named after famous people or historical events; sometimes they have elaborate coats-of-arms, either of some famous person or of a medieval trade guild (or union). Signs can also refer to events in local history or well-known local characters.

The sign for the Royal Oak at Woodchester in Gloucester tells of the famous incident in the Civil War when King Charles hid in an oak tree to escape the Roundhead soldiers who were hunting him below.

The William Caxton commemorates the first man to introduce a printing press into England, and the Plaisterers' Arms has the motto and coat of arms (which shows the tools of their trade) of the plasterers' guild.

The Drunken Duck and the Cook's Ferry Inn both refer to local stories. The sign at Cook's Ferry shows an old man called Matthew Cook who used to ferry people across the river in his boat, before there was a bridge; he was a rather rude and eccentric man and usually had his fourteen cats with him in the boat – much to the disgust of his passengers. The Drunken Duck comes from Hawkshead in the Lake District; the story is told that the landlady one day found her ducks lying in the road, thinking they were dead she began to pluck them ready for eating when the ducks started to move again. She found that a barrel of beer in her cellar had broken and was leaking its contents into the ducks' feeding place. According to local legend the landlady knitted sweaters for the ducks till their feathers grew again.

In a group you can make a survey of the pub signs in your area.

Draw a sketch map to show where each of the pubs is located.

Make a careful drawing of each sign – these drawings can then be turned into finished paintings when you get back to school.

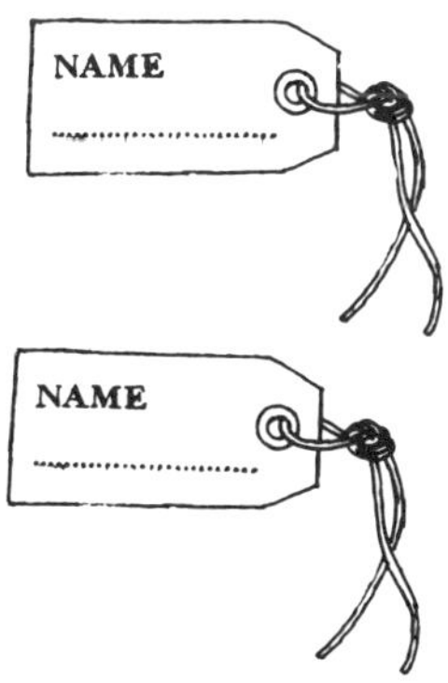

For each of the pub signs in your area, try to find out how the pub got its name. Are there any with a special story to explain the picture? You may need to consult books on the local history of your area to answer some of these questions.

Discuss in a group why you think inn signs had such bright and often detailed pictures on them, as well as having the name of the pub. Remember that when inns started to have signs, shops had picture signs outside as well.

PLANT NAMES

Common plants often have two names: the everyday one which usually describes the plant and the way it grows, such as Busy Lizzie, Mother of Thousands, Mother-in-Law's tongue; and the botanical name in Latin which tells you the family it belongs to and often describes it (for example, the Latin name for Busy Lizzie is Impatiens Balsaminaceae).

Edward Lear took the idea of this long Latin name and made up his own, but in English. Then he drew the plants he had invented.

Nasticreechia Krorluppia

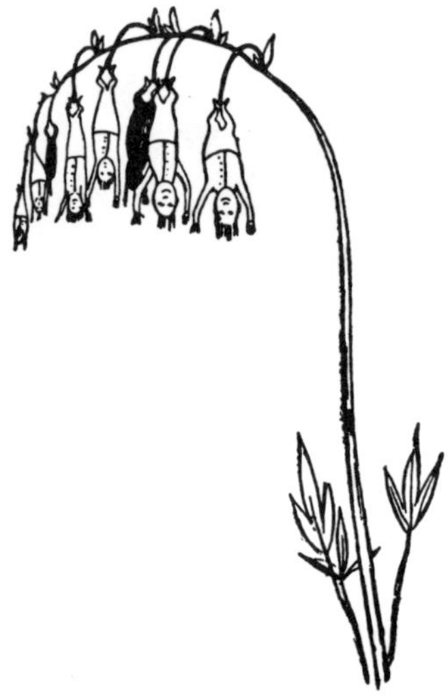

Manypeeplia Upsidownia

Try inventing some plants of your own; draw them and give them suitable names. You could begin by making up drawings to fit some of Edward Lear's other names:

Nasticreechia Krorluppia
Sophtsluggia Glutinosa
Crabbia Horrida
Armchairia Comfortabilis

(you may need to say the names aloud to yourself to help the meaning).

Or you could try some of these to start you off:

Dustbinia Wotapongia
Manypeeplia Outofajobia
Birdsis Singsingia.

TRADE NAMES

A company wants to sell dried tobacco leaves rolled in paper for people to put in their mouths and smoke; it calls its product Embassy, or State Express, or Hamlet, or . . .. Why? What on earth have Embassies to do with dried leaves?

A company wants to sell a car, it calls it Crusader, or Astra, or Cavalier, or Jaguar, or . . .. Why?

A company wants to sell alcohol; they call it Strongbow, or Pink Lady, or White Satin, or . . .. Why?

You run a company which wants to sell a new fast car, or a new washing powder or a new fizzy drink. Which name would you choose for each?

Divide into groups and, between you, decide on the name you would choose for each product to make it sell well.

Which names seem most likely to be successful and why?

Which names might be a total disaster?

The names of products are not always chosen because someone thinks they will sell well, though companies do exist simply to think up names for new products made by other companies!

Some names of products come from their inventors. There *was* a Mr Biro who invented a new sort of writing instrument, a Mr Diesel who invented an engine. It's quite easy to forget that there was, and still is, a Mr Ford who made motor cars or a Mr Rolls and a Mr Royce. Their names have almost become words in their own right.

How many words that were originally people's names can you find in this sentence?

> He was dressed in mackintosh, wellingtons, cashmere cardigan and denim jeans and was eating a sandwich as he watched the rugby.

Just to help you there are four words that come from the names of people – inventors, if you like – and four from the names of places where things were invented. Can you sort them out?

Answers to 'What's for dinner?' on page 24.

Steak and kidney pie
Toad-in-the-hole
Peas
Spinach
Tinned peaches
Ravioli
Liver
Cheese on toast
Tinned tomatoes
Currant pasty
Gooseberries
Jelly and blancmange
Pastry with rolled oats
Plums in juice
Tapioca
Treacle tart
Banana custard

ISBN 0 340 34258 7

First published 1986

Photoset by Rowland Phototypesetting Ltd, Bury St Edmunds, Suffolk

Printed in Hong Kong for
Hodder and Stoughton Educational,
a division of Hodder and Stoughton Ltd,
Mill Road, Dunton Green, Sevenoaks, Kent
by Colorcraft Ltd